© 2005 by Barbour Publishing, Inc.

ISBN 1-59310-130-9

Poem by Rachael Acheson is copyrighted and used by permission.

Illustrations by Heather Castles/Image Zoo.

Published by Barbour Publishing, Inc., P.O. Box 719, Uhrichsville, Ohio 44683,
www.barbourbooks.com

*Our mission is to publish and distribute inspirational products offering exceptional
value and biblical encouragement to the masses.*

Member of the
Evangelical Christian
Publishers Association

Printed in China.
5 4 3 2 1

Home for the Holidays

Rebecca Germany

I wish for you this
time of year
a place to call

home.

Home. . .

How do you recognize it?

. . .a soft chair in a small
apartment where you can put

up your feet.

The four sisters sat knitting away while the December snow fell quietly without, and the fire crackled cheerfully within. It was a comfortable old room, though the carpet was faded and the furniture very plain; for a good picture or two hung on the walls, books filled the recesses, chrysanthemums and Christmas roses bloomed in the windows, and a pleasant atmosphere of home-peace pervaded it.

—FROM *Little Women* BY LOUISA MAY ALCOTT

. . .wherever you surround

yourself with your

favorite things.

"Merry Christmas, little people," she cried in a voice they had not heard in a long time. They both rushed to her and Kate's heart stood still as they each hugged her tight, kissed her, and offered a tiny packet. From the size and feeling of these, she realized that they were giving her the candy they had received the day before at school.

—FROM *Daughter of the Land* BY GENE STRATTON-PORTER

*. . .the fireside at Grandma's
house where the memories are*
as sweet as the cookies.

It comes every year and will go on forever.
And along with Christmas belong the keepsakes and the customs.
Those humble, everyday things a mother clings to, and ponders,
like Mary in the secret spaces of her heart.

—Marjorie Holmes

"I have been reminded of your sincere faith,
which first lived in your grandmother Lois
and in your mother Eunice and,
I am persuaded, now lives in you also."

—2 Timothy 1:5

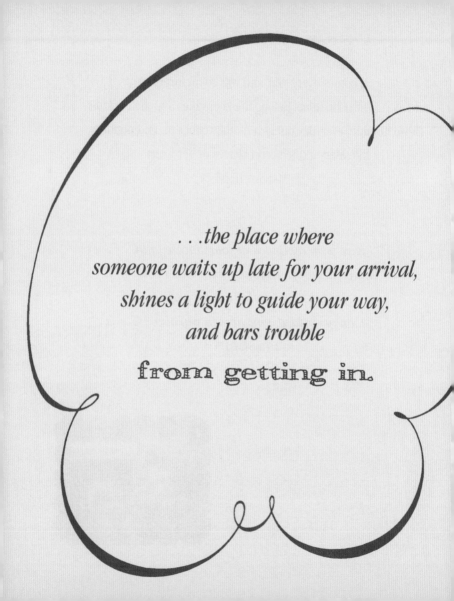

*. . .the place where
someone waits up late for your arrival,
shines a light to guide your way,
and bars trouble*

from getting in.

This is the true nature of home—
it is the place of peace; the shelter, not only from injury,
but from all terror, doubt, and division.

—John Ruskin

e could have cried real tears of wonder and joy as he stood there, gazing. He
t as though he were one of those motion pictures in which a lone Klondiker
s by his campfire cooking a can of salmon or baked beans, and up above
m on the screen in one corner appears the
ristmas tree where his wife and baby at
me are celebrating and missing him. It
emed just as unreal as that to see that
le beautiful home cottage set down in
e midst of the city.

-from *The War Romance of*
e *Salvation Army*
Evangeline Booth and Grace Livingston Hill

. . .the place you
prefer to be when

snowed in.

Christmas morning broke on a beautiful white world. It had been a very mild December and people had looked forward to a green Christmas; but just enough snow fell softly in the night to transfigure Avonlea. Anne peeped out from her frosted gable window with delighted eyes. The firs in the Haunted Wood were all feathery and wonderful; the birches and wild cherry trees were outlined in pearl; the plowed fields were stretches of snowy dimples; and there was a crisp tang in the air that was glorious. Anne ran downstairs singing until her voice reechoed through Green Gables.

—FROM *Anne of Green Gables* BY LUCY MAUD MONTGOMERY

Shut the door. Not that it lets in the cold but that it lets out the coziness.

—MARK TWAIN, *Notebook*, 18

Love keeps the cold out better than a cloak.

—HENRY WADSWORTH LONGFELLOW

Heap on the wood!—the wind is chi

But let it whistle as it wi

We'll keep our Christmas merry sti

—SIR WALTER SCO

Holiday. . .

How do you celebrate it?

Taste

Christmas has more flavor associated with it than any other time of the year. It is the time when food becomes a gift, and family members will go out of their way to make your favorite treat.

Hot Beef Dip

A flavor-filled starter.

¼ cup onion, chopped
1 tablespoon butter
1 (8 ounce) package cream cheese
1 cup milk
1 (4 ounce) can sliced mushrooms
1 (2.5 ounce) package dried beef, chopped
¼ cup Parmesan cheese
2 tablespoons parsley, chopped or dried

a medium saucepan, sauté onion in butter. Add cream cheese and milk;
r until cream cheese melts. Blend in
ushrooms, dried beef, Parmesan, and
rsley. Serve hot with crackers or tortilla
ips. Can be kept warm in a small Crock-
t while serving.

Ribbon Salad

A labor of love.

1 small box cherry or
  orange gelatin
2 small boxes lemon gelatin
2 small boxes lime gelatin

2 small boxes black
  raspberry gelatin
4 cups boiling water
2 cups sour cream

In a mixing bowl, dissolve cherry or orange gelatin in 1 cup of boiling water. Separate into 2 bowls, ½ cup each. To one portion, add ½ cup sour cream and whip; pour on the bottom of a 9x13 pan and chill until set. To other portion of cherry gelatin, add 3 teaspoons of cold water. Pour on top of first layer of set gelatin. Repeat this layering process with each box of gelatin. Each layer will take 20–30 minutes to set, so the complete process takes time, but the end result is well worth the fuss.

Old-Fashioned Sugar Cookies

An antique recipe with great reliable taste—lard is the secret.

3 eggs, beaten
2 teaspoons vanilla
2 cups sugar
1 cup lard or shortening

1 cup milk
½ teaspoon baking soda
7 cups flour (approximately)
4 teaspoons baking powder

Mix eggs, vanilla, sugar, and lard until smooth. Blend milk and baking soda together before adding it to the mixture. Sift together flour and baking powder, then slowly add to the mixture until the dough is the right texture for handling. Roll dough out on a floured surface and cut into shapes with cookie cutters. Bake for 10 minutes at 350 degrees.

Cookie Truffles

This is easy and looks great!

1 pound package of chocolate sandwich cookies, crushed
1 (8 ounce) package cream cheese, softened
1 pound chocolate candy coating, melted
¼ cup white candy coating or white chocolate chips, melted

In a large mixing bowl, combine crushed cookies and cream cheese to form a stiff dough. Shape into balls then dip with a fork into melted candy coating. Place on a wire rack over waxed paper in a cool area until set. Decorate the top with white chocolate. Melt the candy in a plastic bag, cut a tiny hole in one corner, and drizzle over the top of each candy ball.

Family

There is something about this time of year that draws family and loved ones together on a pilgrimage to the foot of the old Christmas tree. But Christmas is not in the tree, or the wreath, or the lights, or the cookies. . . . Christmas is an opportunity to put to rest the troubles from throughout the year and start afresh with a new display of love for one another— **because one kind word at Christmastime can warm a soul for three long winter months.**

A Magical Christmas Eve

We crept from out our bed that night,
My sister Liz and I,
And tiptoed through the silent halls
The Christmas tree to spy.

We clasped each other's chilly hands
As though we feared the dark
Which barred our sight, would bid
The other sibling to depart.

There stood our glorious Christmas tree
Encased in magic shine;
And thrilled with quiet joy were we
Beside the glittering shrine.

No conversation did we make
For fear our parents would awake,
But sat beside that gorgeous tree
And drank its tuneless melody.

We sat, I do not know how long,
'Til drowsiness our eyes consumed
And each, in dimming wonder, thought
Of soon returning to our rooms.

But all at once, in sweet appeal,
My sister's arm round me I feel;
I hear her whisper once again
The words bestowed on me just then:

"Merry Christmas!" My heart was warm
As she nestled her head against my arm.
I thought to myself I would never forget
Our secret adventure's tender summit.

For when she spoke, I felt the darkness
Of the night was worn,
And was replaced, as we went to bed,
By the birth of Christmas morn.

—RACHAEL ACHESON © 2004

God sets the lonely
in families.

—Psalm 68:6

Without a family, man, alone in the world, trembles with the col...

—Andre Mauro...

Our hearts grow tender with childhood memories and love of kindred,
and we are better throughout the year for having, in spirit,
become a child again at Christmastime.

—Laura Ingalls Wilder

He that raises a large family does, indee...

while he lives to observe them, stand a broader mark for sorro...

but then he stands a broader mark for pleasure to...

—Benjamin Frankl...

Love

Christmas is expressed through giving, and giving is how we show our love for others. It is most easy to give to those we love, but the greatest joy is when we can extend God's love by giving to strangers in need.

For the first, and greatest, gift of love was that while we were still trapped in our sins, Christ entered this world as a baby and gave His life to redeem ours (Romans 5:8).

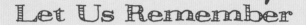

Let Us Remember

And when we give each other Christmas gifts in His Name,
let us remember that He has given us the sun and the moon and the stars,
and the earth with its forests and mountains and oceans—
and all that lives and moves upon them.
He has given us all green things
and everything that blossoms and bears fruit—
and all that we quarrel about and all that we have misused—
and to save us from our own foolishness, from all our sins,
He came down to earth and gave us Himself.

—SIGRID UNDSET

Somehow not only for Christmas but all the long year through,
the joy that you give to others is the joy that comes back to you.
And the more you spend in blessing the poor and lonely and sad,
the more of your heart's possessing returns to make you glad.

—JOHN GREENLEAF WHITTIER

Christmas, my child,
is love in action. . . .
Every time we love,
every time we give,
it's Christmas.

—DALE EVANS ROGERS

ou can give without loving,
ut you cannot love without giving.

—AMY CARMICHAEL

Christmas is

not a time nor a season,
but a state of mind.
To cherish peace and goodwill,
to be plenteous in mercy,
is to have the real spirit of Christmas.

—CALVIN COOLIDGE

seems ironic that we can't wait to get to that place we call home to celebrate Christmas within the circle of family love—but what we are really celebrating is the time when God's Son left the comforts of His heavenly home to come to a cold, cruel world to be rejected, left homeless, and scorned for our sake. **That is the essence of true Christmas love!**

Going Home for Christmas

Are you going home for Christmas? Have you written you'll be there?
Going home to kiss the mother and to show her that you care?
Going home to greet the father in a way to make him glad?
If you're not I hope there'll never come a time you'll wish you had.
Just sit down and write a letter—it will make their heart strings hum
With a tune of perfect gladness—if you'll tell them that you'll come.

—Edgar Albert Guest